# contents....

## Autistic spectrum disorders

The publication *Autistic Spectrum Disorders: Good Practice Guidance* (DfES 2002) highlights the need for greater understanding of autistic spectrum disorders and in the provision that is made for children with these conditions and their families. Consequently the education service has recognised that there is a need for specific advice to support staff working with pupils with an autistic spectrum disorder (ASD) in secondary schools and therefore, in consultation with colleagues from North Bristol NHS Trust, South Gloucestershire Inclusion Support Service has produced these guidelines.

These guidelines have been written to help support colleagues in promoting the inclusion of these pupils in mainstream schools in South Gloucestershire. Pupils with an ASD bring to the school qualities unique to the person with an ASD which should be valued and, where possible, accommodated.

Van Krevelen (cited in Wing 1991) noted that the low-functioning pupil with autism 'lives in a world of his own', whereas the higher functioning pupil with autism 'lives in our world but in his own way.'

Greater understanding of their differences in learning style and social interaction will promote effective inclusion.

We hope that greater understanding of differences in learning styles and social interaction will promote effective inclusion, and that all staff carrying out an invaluable role working with young people with an ASD will find the material useful.

*Jane C. Spouse*

Jane Spouse
Deputy Director for Children and Young People

Wing, L (1991) Language, Social and Cognitive Impairments in Autism and Severe Mental Retardation, *Journal of Autism and Developmental Disorders Vol. 11*

# Guidelines for working with pupils with an autistic spectrum disorder in key stages 3 and 4

South Gloucestershire Council Department for Children and Young People

# acknowledgements....

**Guidelines for working with pupils with an Autistic Spectrum Disorder in Key Stages 3 and 4**

## Authors

Eryl Daniels     *SEN Support Network Manager*

Mark Hamlin     *Educational Psychologist*

Sally Hewison     *Specialist Speech and Language Therapist for Children with Complex Communication Needs*

Sue Fairhurst     *Senior Educational Psychologist*

## Acknowledgements

We would like to thank colleagues from central support services and schools for their support with the preparation of these guidelines. Also many thanks to the parents of the local Branch of The National Autistic Society for their advice and suggestions. And lastly to the pupils from Filton High School Resource Base for their cartoons.

# what is
# Autistic spectrum disorder....

Autistic spectrum disorder (ASD) is a complex developmental disability that lasts throughout life. It affects more boys than girls and includes the syndromes described by Kanner and Asperger.

ASD affects the way a person communicates, relates to people and understands the world around them. These difficulties are referred to as 'the triad of impairments,' although many now prefer that they should be known as 'the triad of differences.' For a diagnosis to be made, specific types and degrees of difference must be present in each of the three areas:

● social interaction
● social communication
● imagination – flexibility of thought

Children with autism vary greatly, as the effects of autism can be mild or severe and be influenced by age, personality, life experiences and any other disability the child may have. Most children with autism will have moderate or severe learning difficulties and up to half may not learn to use spoken language. Those with Asperger syndrome have fewer problems with language and are less likely to have additional learning difficulties, although they often experience problems with communication and motor skills.

Most young people with Asperger syndrome attend a mainstream school.  As a result of the core differences, the problems with motor skills and unusual responses to sensory stimuli, children with Asperger syndrome often experience a range of significant difficulties in school.

Adolescents with an ASD are at higher risk of experiencing depression. However, pupils with Asperger syndrome can also have considerable strengths eg a good memory for facts, good perseverance and focus on subjects of particular interest and advanced knowledge of some area of technology or science.

Due to the wide variation in the difficulties experienced within the school setting, there has to be a corresponding variation in the provision made for pupils with an ASD. Some require no additional support or resources whilst others may have a Statement of Special Educational Need and have a variety of different types and amounts of support.

The guidance within this booklet should help you to understand the individual needs and behaviour of pupils with an ASD, as well as to tailor the support provided for each individual. **Many of the strategies that have proved effective in helping pupils with an ASD may also help other pupils who are experiencing difficulties in relation to social, organisation and communication skills.**

# implications of an ASD for pupils in key stages 3 and 4...

Each of the three areas of difference – social interaction, social communication and imagination – has implications for a pupil's ability to be included in all aspects of school life.

## Social interaction

Pupils who have an ASD will have **difficulties interpreting and using the unwritten rules of social interaction.** This means that pupils will have difficulty understanding the intent of peers and adults at school.

*A collision in a busy corridor may be interpreted as aggression.*

Pupils with an ASD may **wish to have friends** and to mix socially with their peers. Pupils may appear to be on the edge of social groups. However, because of their social differences, they may behave in an inappropriate way, for example, asking personal questions which they may have heard others asking close friends in a more socially acceptable way. This may result in sympathy from some peers and/or may make pupils a target for bullying. Initially sympathetic peers may distance themselves from the pupil to avoid negative attention from others.

Pupils with an ASD may have **difficulty with empathy** and so find it difficult to recognise how another person is feeling.

*Pupils may not 'read' the teacher's signal – tone of voice, facial expression, eye gaze. They will not see that the teacher is getting increasingly cross with the pupil's repeated interruptions until the teacher shouts.*

This contrasts with pupils who have an awareness of the effect of their actions in deliberately 'winding up' the teacher or another pupil. Pupils with an ASD may also not show their own feelings by conventional means when they feel upset so there may be little warning before an outburst.

Pupils with an ASD are different from pupils who are rebellious or 'naughty.' They do not have the awareness of social conventions. The rebellious pupil is aware of the conventions and chooses to challenge them.

Pupils with an ASD may be very aware that they are different and try hard to fit in. This requires enormous effort and can result in high levels of anxiety, which may be apparent in the pupil's behaviour (eg reliance on particular items of interest or rituals), or this may not be apparent until an outburst occurs.

The impact of the differences in social interaction, communication and imagination on pupils with an ASD depend on the response of other people to the pupil. Within schools, particularly larger secondary schools, pupils mix with a wide variety of adults and peers, who potentially have only limited knowledge of the nature and impact of these differences.

In addition to this, the social environment of a large secondary school can be more challenging for pupils who are socially naive.

## Social communication

Pupils with an ASD may have a **different communication style** to other pupils. They may have a speech style that does not fit into the social context of the community. Some pupils may have unusual intonation, for example, an 'American' accent, or very flat prosody (speaking in a monotone). Pupils may have **poor awareness of the social hierarchy** that exists in some schools that may dictate which style to use with which person.

*The pupils' communication style may be appropriate with many staff, but not when chatting to peers, eg they may talk to the headteacher using vocabulary which is appropriate between friends at break, but not with staff.*

Pupils with an ASD have difficulties in non-verbal interaction and may have difficulties with conversational turn-taking, eye gaze, body language, and proximity. These difficulties can be detrimental to relationships with peers and can be experienced as threatening, aggressive or inappropriate. Difficulties with reciprocal interaction, for example, conversational turn-taking and awareness of the listener's needs have implications for both social and academic attainment, and make working in pairs or groups very challenging for pupils with an ASD and their peers. Pupils with an ASD may talk repetitively about their own particular interests.

*When asked where they went on holiday, pupils with an ASD might give a detailed description of all the roads and signposts passed but not share the name of the town.*

Some pupils with an ASD have **difficulty understanding spoken language**. This might be because they have a language impairment and do not understand concepts or grammar or may have difficulty remembering language. Other pupils may have difficulty identifying when language is addressed to them, so they find it very difficult to screen out all the language that they do not need to process.

Finally, most pupils with an ASD have **difficulty understanding less literal language** (eg metaphor, irony and verbal humour). This may result in pupils who seem to have good understanding having unexpected difficulties. Pupils with difficulties understanding non-literal language may not make the inference required to understand the intent of the speaker.

| What is said | What is intended |
|---|---|
| Look at page 14 | and read it |
| Do you know where the office is? | take it there |
| It's nearly breaktime | Hurry up! |
| Are you listening? | Listen |
| I'll pick you up later | I'll meet you and take you there |
| Are you ready? | Get ready |
| See me | Come to my desk when the other pupils are working |
| Have I got your homework? | Give me your homework |

Some pupils with Asperger syndrome can be taught about non-literal language and, once they have understood the idea of words not meaning quite what they say, they may get a great deal of pleasure from 'playing' with language.

Many pupils with Asperger syndrome may have **good mechanical reading skills**, which may hide their **poor understanding of text (hyperlexia).**

## Imagination — flexibility of thought

Some people with ASD can become **very focused on maintaining sameness**. Within any community life is not entirely predictable and this can be a particularly difficult for pupils who have an ASD. Every person that they come into contact with can and does change their clothes, voice and mood on a regular basis without necessarily having much awareness of these differences. A change in classroom, a supply teacher or not being able to find the correct pen can be enough to prevent pupils concentrating and may cause a great deal of anxiety.

Pupils with an ASD will find it **difficult to imagine or pretend** and this can affect many areas of the curriculum.

*They can find it difficult to:*
- *understand fiction and poetry*
- *write stories*
- *imagine what it was like when...*
- *make predictions*
- *respond flexibly to the unexpected (eg a firebell at dinner time, rather than during a lesson when it had been practised)*
- *test the limits (eg might be more likely to use equipment exactly as taught, rather than experimenting with different methods)*
- *differentiate between fact and fiction*
- *evaluate text/events etc*
- *understand that '1' can mean different amounts depending on place (eg 1, 10, 100, 1000 etc) and that x is unknown.*

However some pupils with an ASD have a **huge amount of factual knowledge about their particular interest**.

Pupils **may not respond to the same motivators as their peers.**

Whole school house point systems are not likely to be motivating as pupils are unlikely to identify with their own house and so will not work hard to get points to help beat the other houses.

Many pupils are not motivated by the teacher's praise but might be more motivated by a concrete system that results in winning time on a preferred activity on a regular basis (eg exploring the cartoon network website).

Many pupils with an ASD are **hypersensitive to sensory stimuli**. This can be touch, sound, taste, smell and/or sight. This may result in apparently inappropriate responses to ordinary stimuli.

Pupils may be **very distractible** due to heightened awareness of sensory stimuli. Other distractors could be their own thought processes (related to topic of particular interest) and/or lack of awareness of their membership of the class group.

## Motor co-ordination

Many pupils with ASD have **poor motor skills**. This can affect their ability to participate in games and PE, their handwriting speed, presentation and accuracy and therefore completion of homework. Many pupils find it difficult to copy homework quickly and accurately from the board and then, when they attempt the homework, they – and their parents – are unable to make sense of the task. Pupils may also produce less written work than peers, despite the same time and effort.

Pupils with an ASD are likely to have **poor personal organisation**, so that they may arrive at lessons late and/or with the wrong equipment.

# summary....

Although the main areas of difference have been dealt with separately, it is clear that there is a great deal of overlap, and that the difficulties have a tendency to compound each other. In addition, as pupils reach adolescence, the expectations of family, school and society change.

The very nature of the difficulties experienced by pupils with ASD make it difficult for pupils to understand and cope with both the physical and emotional changes of adolescence and the changes in expectation of the people around them. This makes these pupils particularly vulnerable to anxiety and depression.

**Far more boys than girls have Asperger syndrome. Because of this and to simplify this book, the term 'he' has been used throughout.**

# In class

These tips are ways of working with pupils with an ASD. Not all are appropriate for every pupil. You need to get to know your pupil first. However, many of these tips will be helpful with all pupils.

## Classroom and learning environment

Pupils with ASDs like routine and structure therefore, the more predictable the learning environment, the more likely it is that they will cope with demands and be less likely to experience stress. Remember: stress presents as challenging or inappropriate behaviour.

## Tips

- Think about the most appropriate seating position for a pupil with an ASD:
  - facing the board or focus of attention
  - near the teacher
  - near positive role models
  - away from distractions (eg doorway, windows, displays)
  - alongside supportive peers.

  It may be helpful to provide the same place for each lesson. If working in different rooms, determine a seating place for each room.
- Organise the teaching room, especially specialist rooms, so that it guides the pupil to meeting expectations.
  - Is equipment labelled and accessible?
  - Does the pupil with ASD need to be provided with the essential equipment such as pen, pencil, ruler etc?
  - Remove unwanted or unnecessary books/equipment.
- Be clear about the structure of the lesson – starter, main part and plenary.
- Write the purpose/aim of the lesson on the board to help the pupil 'tune in' to the lesson.
- Teach **visually** as far as possible.
- Structure the learning activities into small tasks, making clear the beginning and end of each task.
- Say precisely what is expected; what work, how much and when to stop.
- Give warning of when to stop.
- Be aware that these pupils may be hypersensitive to stimuli – light, noise, touch, heat etc.

## Understanding the language and following instructions

A pupil with an ASD will probably understand the individual words you use but may not interpret the message of what you are saying. They find it hard to figure out what is relevant information.

> 'My hearing is like having a hearing aid with the volume control stuck on 'super loud'. It is like an open microphone that picks up everything. I have two choices: turn the mike on and be deluged with sound, or shut off. Mother reported that I sometimes acted like I was deaf.'

## Tips

- Just prior to a whole class listening activity or watching a video, give the pupil or all pupils a prompt sheet with the key points or key words for which to watch and listen (Appendix 1).

- Pupils with ASD may not follow class instructions unless you cue them in. Say the pupil's name first, **pause** and then, give the instruction.
  'James, ................ listen to what I am going to say.'

- Think about your language when giving instructions – simplify language and say precisely what you mean.

- Avoid indirect instructions such as *'Can you tidy away?'* Instead say *'Put your books in your bag.'*

  Avoid instructions such as *'Look at page 6'* which implies *'....and read the words.'*

### Be explicit.

- Give one instruction at a time, not a sequence.

- Give positive instructions to tell the pupil what you want them to do:
  *'Fold your arms'* rather than *'Stop fiddling with your pen.'*

- Encourage eye contact but do not insist upon it. For a person with an ASD looking and listening are separate activities, so if a pupil is to listen, do not insist on them maintaining eye contact.

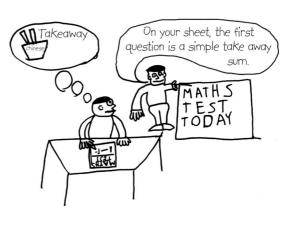

- Encourage the pupil to look towards the person talking.

- Teach new vocabulary, especially specialist vocabulary, remembering that some words have a different meaning depending on the context, for example, takeaway, ruler.

- Back up verbal instructions with written ones: use keyword lists or highlight keywords in text.

- Use visual supports to aid understanding of language: pictures, symbols, diagrams, flow charts, word maps or concept maps. (Appendix 2)

## Adults' use of language

The pupil may have superficially good spoken language but he may use it very literally. Good language or vocabulary can mask lack of understanding.

# Tips

- Avoid sarcasm or metaphors, *'I could eat a horse.'*

- If metaphors are used in a subject, they will need to be explained.

- Be careful with expressions like *'Pull your socks up'* as they can cause confusion.

- Do not assume that pupils with an ASD understand something because they repeat back what they have heard. **Check understanding.**

- Be aware that the pupils with an ASD may appear rude if they respond literally.

- Be careful with comments to a pupil with ASD. Some comments may cause confusion.

## Learning style

Pupils with ASDs approach things differently, therefore, they have a different style of learning.

## Tips

- Pupils with an ASD may have advanced skills in certain areas, e.g. rote learning, drawing skills, computational skills, decoding or memory, capitalising on their strengths.

- Additional structure will be needed with creative work. Tasks or assignments will need to be broken into small steps with frequent adult input.

- Pupils with an ASD often find it hard to generalise learning from one context to another. They therefore need plenty of over-learning taught in a range of contexts.

- Provide pupils with a worksheet, a cloze text, a writing frame, a list of questions and/or keywords to support the recording of ideas.

- Some pupils with an ASD may have difficulties with recording work or be obsessed with neatness. Consider alternative methods of recording work – ICT, tape, cloze procedures, diagrams and cartoons. Give more time to complete assignments.

- Encourage pupils to ask for clarification by teaching them how to ask for help. For example, tell them to put their hand up and say *'I don't understand'* or give them an agreed signal. Writing a Social Story™ can help to teach the appropriate action. (Appendix 3)

- Give advance warning of changes to routine or change of learning activity. Again, making explicit the structure of the lesson can help the pupil to move on from one activity to the next.

- Make clear the purpose of the task. Pupils with an ASD may not engage in the task unless they know why, for example, practising a mastered skill once they have done it!

- Be aware that pupils with an ASD may give the correct answer but be unable to explain how they reached it.

- Pupils with an ASD may be motivated:
  - by understanding the purpose of the task
  - having a particular interest
  - receiving a reward of value to them.

Pupils with ASD may not respond to the usual rewards and you will need to ask them what works for them. Special interests may be used as rewards, eg internet research or drawing.

- Pupils with an ASD have difficulties with empathy. For example, difficulties with understanding the perspectives and experiences of different people or cultures may impact upon many areas of the curriculum.

- Group work may be difficult for pupils with an ASD. Try to find an appropriate partner, assign specific roles to the pupils and be explicit about expectations and outcomes.

- Tests and exams are strange social situations. Prepare the pupils in advance.

- Homework and school are two different places, so the idea of homework may be difficult.

- Homework needs to be checked in the log/diary to see if it is recorded accurately with the purpose clearly explained. Is the parent going to understand what to do?

  - It may help to set up a homework buddy, making sure at the start of the year/term that there is a note of the buddy's phone number in the diary.

  - Consider giving pupils with an ASD a dictaphone for teachers to record homework.

  - Write the homework on a slip of paper in advance and stick into the diary.

  - Establish a homework club in school and encourage pupils to attend.

- Be aware that the content of homework may be difficult for the pupil. They may answer well in class but then find it difficult to re-use that learning in a different setting. They may recall the facts well (good rote memory) but not be able to apply the knowledge.

- Pupils with an ASD may experience difficulties with motor skills. They may be clumsy and awkward. They may have difficulties with fine motor skills, which affect handwriting and presentation.

- Investigate the possibility of giving an alternative to PE for pupils with an ASD. For example, participating in a health/fitness curriculum (trampoline, running or swimming) rather than competitive sports. Pupils with ASD may also lack the social understanding of co-ordinating one's own actions with those of others in a team.

- If gross motor problems are severe, seek advice from SENCO, Occupational Therapy or Physiotherapy Services.

- Take into account the slow handwriting when setting timed tasks.

- Provide/encourage the use of ICT to aid recording of work.

# Lesson tips.........

**Try remembering these tips when planning a lesson or discussing support with a teaching assistant. Of course all these tips cannot be used in every lesson and you may think of others to add.**

- Think about where a pupil sits.

- Make clear purpose of lesson.

- Write title/topic/keywords/lesson objective on board.

- Language, especially instructions: keep it short and simple (KISS).

- Use clear unambiguous sentences.

- Provide the pupil with ASD with relevant materials:
    - Highlighted text
    - Photocopy of materials
    - Diagrams
    - Pictures/resource books

- At the start of a whole class activity, 'tune' the ASD pupil in by saying his name. Use a visual prompt sheet and help pupil recognise relevant information (Appendix 1).

- Warn the pupil with ASD that you will ask him questions about the topic. Give time for him to process information.

- Give the pupil with ASD the chance to participate – ask questions that you know he can answer.

- Ask questions to check understanding.

- State clearly the task – be specific:
    - Where to start?
    - What to do first, next, last?
    - When to finish?
    - What is the expected outcome?

- Write on the board a visual reminder of the sequence/nature of task, using word list or symbols.

- Give the pupil with ASD a specific role and task when working with a partner or in a small group.

- Give the pupil with ASD keywords, list of questions or visual prompt sheet (Appendix 1) before watching the video/DVD.

- Check homework is recorded accurately.

These lesson tips will help **all** the pupils in the class.

# Around school

All staff, whether subject, pastoral or support, need to be aware of the social interaction difficulties that pupils with an ASD experience and be prepared to actively support them and their peers.

Pupils with an ASD who are new to the school may find the environment noisy, large, unpredictable and confusing. The following suggestions may help to prepare and introduce the pupils with ASD to their new school environment.

- Arrange a meeting with people from the previous school with 'key' staff in order to share information on successful and unsuccessful strategies.

- Meet with parents to learn from their knowledge of ASD and of their child.

- Identify a 'key' person to provide a mentor role for the pupil. It is critical that adolescents have an identified person with whom they can check in at least once daily.

- Try to avoid surprises – prepare pupils in advance for special activities or changes in timetable/routine, no matter how trivial the change.

- Identify a plan for introducing pupils with an ASD to their new school:

  - Where possible, allow pupils to visit the school beforehand out of school hours to familiarise themselves to the layout.

  - Provide a timetable, either written or pictorial (Appendix 4).
    It may help to colour code subjects.

  - Introduce pupils to key staff (Form tutor, SENCO, mentor, head of year).

  - Tell pupils where to go/what to do for help – for example, mentor or school office. (There will be a need to inform office staff).

  - Show the pupils the toilets and explain when they should go.

  - Show the pupils where to go and how to get their school lunch.
    Inform and advise lunchtime staff of the pupils' needs.

  - Provide a list of the school rules, simplified, if possible.

- Plan what to say to their peers. This needs to be done sensitively and in consultation with the pupils and the parents.

  - Talk to peers about the difficulties pupils with an ASD may face. Do not use terms such as ASD, autism or Asperger syndrome as they can become labels. Instead focus on their difficulties – understanding how other people think or feel, understanding rules or what to do in situations.

  - Emphasise the strengths and skills of pupils with an ASD and how they might be helpful to others, eg ICT skills, rote memory or drawing skills.

  - Praise peers when they treat a pupil with an ASD with understanding and respect.

Pupils with an ASD experience difficulties in understanding social situations. They may be vulnerable to bullying because they appear odd, behave inappropriately or may be loners.

- Set up a buddy system.

- Establish a Circle of Friends for the pupil. (Appendix 5)

- Allocate time each week when pupils meet with their mentors to talk through problems and to discuss ways to overcome them.

- Use Visual Scripts or Social Stories™ to help the pupils develop an understanding of social situations (Appendices 3 and 6).

- Provide group work to follow a specific social skills programme. Seek advice from the SENCO, educational psychologist or Behaviour Support Service.

Remember that pupils with an ASD experience difficulties with social interaction and social communication. Therefore, unstructured times, such as break and lunchtimes can be when the pupils are at their most vulnerable. Most pupils consider break and lunchtimes as the best part of the school day but for pupils with an ASD, it can be the most challenging! They have an additional curriculum to learn – the social rules of the classroom and the playground.

- Provide a 'safe haven' – somewhere to go to be themselves. Some pupils with an ASD need a safe place to 'relax' in order to cope with the social demands of the rest of the school day.

- Encourage participation in clubs such as library, ICT room or a chess club.

- Look out for bullying.

# Staff

Secondary schools are large and busy environments, so communication between teachers and support staff can be difficult. It can be hard to find time to talk with colleagues from the same department, let alone other colleagues. However, it is essential that all teaching and support staff have some time together to discuss their concerns and successes.

## Tips

- Plan termly meetings so that all staff exchange information about working with pupils with an ASD – successes and failures – to determine consistent and appropriate strategies.

- A consistent approach across subject areas can help pupils with an ASD understand aspects of school life, eg how pupils are greeted when they enter the classroom or expectations on how to set out work.

- In advance of the lesson, subject teachers and support staff should agree their respective roles and, wherever possible, the support staff should be told about the work.

- Inform supply teachers of pupils with an ASD in their classes.

# Parents — working in partnership with parents

Parents of pupils with an ASD have considerable knowledge about autistic spectrum disorders and of course about their child. Use their knowledge.

Remember that pupils with an ASD have difficulty with communication and so parents do not get any information about what is happening at school. It is hard enough to get information from any adolescent but from an adolescent with an ASD it is even harder!

Also consider that the families of pupils with an ASD are likely to be under considerable stress.

## Tips

- It is vital that schools establish and maintain contact with the parents of pupils with an ASD. Invite them into school, especially when the pupils are new to the school.

- Give parents a contact name – this may be the Head of Year, tutor or support teacher but make sure that parents know whom to contact with any queries or concerns. Advise when best to telephone. Minor problems do not need to become a crisis!

- Provide the parents with copies of the school and homework timetables, school rules and even a plan of the school. This allows them to go over things at home.

- Use the school diary/planner to send messages home/ share information, eg write in it what is needed for the next DT lesson.

- Avoid contacting parents only when there is a crisis. Seek parents' involvement when there are minor problems so that they can help in finding solutions and adopting complementary practices at home.

- Let parents know when things are going well – particular successes. Remember: a pupil with an ASD may not communicate the good news!

- Give the parents a copy of the programme of work, syllabus or text books at the start of each term so that they can understand the context of the work.

- Try to inform parents of any changes to the school routine so that they can forewarn the pupils. It may only be a slight change but small incidents can cause problems for the pupils with ASD and at home for the parents.

# behaviour....

**Remember: behaviour problems in pupils with an ASD are rarely deliberate and should not be described as 'naughtiness.' Challenging or inappropriate behaviours are usually a communication of anxiety or stress. Many can be avoided by ensuring that the pupils understand what is required or what changes are about to occur.**

You may observe pupils with an ASD showing the first signs of stress (minor behaviour problems such as tense muscles, fidgety, complaining of feeling ill, shouting out, challenging you or beginning to lash out).

Try one of the following:

- Remove pupils from the situation by sending them on out an 'errand', eg to the office. The opportunity for time out of the classroom may give the pupil time to calm before returning to class.

- Create and use a safe 'home base', perhaps in the learning support department – a place where they may go to regain control.

- Encourage pupils to complete work in a less stressful environment.

- Establish a signal with them as to when to go, eg handing over an exit or red card.

- Restate your request:
  - be brief and simple
  - back up what you say with any visual system
  - keep your style low key – speak in a quiet, calm but firm voice and do not move in a threatening manner.

- Acknowledge a problem, eg if the pupil complains in maths that the work is too hard say, *'Yes, it is difficult. Please do number 1.'*

- Make a slightly different and smaller demand, one that the pupil is likely to do.

- Do not expect/ask for a direct response or an answer. Give the pupil with ASD time and space to make sense of what is asked.

- If the behaviour becomes more challenging, ask the pupil with ASD to follow you outside. Turn and walk out of room. The adult should just walk with the pupil without talking. Allow the pupil to say whatever they want. Use the support staff for this strategy: *'Just walk, don't talk.'*

If it has not been possible to defuse the pupil's stress and so his behaviour, then there needs to be a plan on how to handle the situation. Be clear about who should be involved, when and who takes the lead. Try to remain as calm as possible.

After an outburst/incident, give the pupil space to calm down. The pupil may continue to feel very anxious, so do not rush to talk it through. Try to get back to normal as soon as possible by helping him to become part of the class routine again. If possible, find something that the pupil can do which can be praised.

Afterwards provide time for the pupil to talk through the incident. It may be possible to gain information about the situation from the pupil's perspective that can help in preventing a repetition in the future:

- try to avoid blame
- focus on the 'facts' as the pupil sees them
- try to ignore accusations and try to resolve the crisis
- focus on the 'what' of the behaviour rather than the 'why.'

Following an incident 'key' staff should meet to try to determine ways of reducing the anxiety and enabling the pupil with an ASD to cope. Consider the **STAR** approach.

- **S**etting in which the problem occurs
- **T**riggers or events that seem to set off the problem
- **A**ction – what the pupil actually does
- **R**esults of behaviour – the effects it has and what it seems to achieve for the pupil.

Observation focusing on this approach can help to identify the factors that may be changed to bring about improvements in behaviour.

(STAR record sheet Appendix 7)

# good practice guidelines....

This is taken from DfES (2002) *Autistic Spectrum Disorders Good Practice Guidelines*, which schools may use to check their current practice and then plan any developments.

**An ASD friendly school should:**

- make sure all teachers are aware of their duties under the SEN Code of Practice to identify children's needs, including those with ASDs

- have a named person, possibly the SENCO, who can provide guidance on ASDs and ensure that all staff who come into contact with a child with an ASD are aware of the particular needs of that child

- encourage staff with knowledge and experience of children with ASDs to share their expertise with any existing outreach support teams and with other school staff

- keep an up-to-date bank of information on ASDs for use by staff and parents

- have a policy on working with children with an ASD and keep up-to-date records of staff ASD training

- consult specialist staff (Outreach Support teams if available within the LEA) when developing policies on ASDs

- make sure a named member of staff who knows about ASDs is available to discuss any concerns the child with an ASD may have and help the child to contribute as fully as possible to the development of their provision

- ensure the curriculum of the child with an ASD is tailored to meet their needs

- provide opportunities for children with an ASD to generalise skills learnt in one setting/lesson to other situations/settings

- recognise that ICT can be a particularly effective medium for children with an ASD

- modify the school environment to take account of the difficulties with sensory stimuli experienced by some children with ASDs

- work closely with parents and families, consulting them about Individual Educational Plans (IEPs) and Behaviour Plans and inviting them to join in with ASD training where appropriate

- support families by ensuring that out-of-school activities include provision for children with ASDs

- develop communication networks between the LEA and Health and Social Services Departments, so that there is a three way flow of information, regarding individual children with an ASD, and a three way flow of up to date information regarding ASD policy and practice

- ensure smooth transition between settings by exchanging accurate and up to date records, profiles and ways of working with the child with an ASD

- work closely with the Connexions Services (careers advisors) to ensure a smooth transition to Post-16 provision for pupils with an ASD.

# where can you get help.....

**Should you need or want to know more consider the following:-**

- For further advice contact the Educational Psychologist (EP) via the SENCO who then may involve an external agency such as Inclusion Support Service (ISS), Speech and Language Therapy Service (SLTS), Behaviour Support Service (BSS) or Child and Adolescent Mental Health Services (CAMHS).

- Look in the Continuing Professional Development booklet or the National Autistic website for further training.

- Within South Gloucestershire attend Communication Network Meetings – look out for the termly Newsletter or ask your SENCO for details.
  - A library of specialist resources is available from the Communication Network.

- Contact The National Autistic Society (NAS)
  393 City Road, London EC1V 1NG
  Tel: 020 7833 2299
  Helpline: 0845 070 4004
  Email: nas@nas.org.uk  autismhelpline@nas.org.uk

- **Useful websites:**  www.autism.org.uk   www.info.autism.org.uk   www.autismuk.com

- **Useful titles**

  **General overview of ASDs**

  *Attwood, T (1998) *Asperger's syndrome; a guide for parents and professionals.* London, Jessica Kingsley

  *Clements, J and Zarkowska, E (2000) *Behavioural concerns and autistic spectrum disorders: explanations and strategies for change.*  London: Jessica Kingsley Publishers

  *Leicester City Council and Leicestershire County Council (1998) *Asperger syndrome – practical strategies for the classroom: a teacher's guide.* London: The National Autistic Society

  *Hesmondhalgh, M and Breakey, C (2001) *Let me in: access and inclusion for children with autistic spectrum disorders.* London: Jessica Kingsley Publishers

  *Welton, J (2004) *What did you say? What do you mean? An illustrated guide to understanding metaphors.* London: Jessica Kingsley Publications

  *Whitaker, P (2001) *Challenging behaviour and autism: making sense – making progress.* London: The National Autistic Society

**Personal Perspectives from people with an ASD**

*Sainsbury, C (2000) *Martian in the playground.* Bristol, Lucky Duck Publishing

- **Booklets**

  *Colley, J (2004) *Working with an Asperger pupil in secondary schools.* London: The National Autistic Society

  *Thorpe, P (2003) *Moving from primary to secondary school: guidelines for pupils with autistic spectrum disorder.* London: The National Autistic Society

  *Thorpe, P (2004) *Understanding difficulties during break time and lunchtime at secondary school: guidelines for pupils with autistic spectrum disorders.* London: The National Autistic Society

- **Videos**

  *A is for Autism.* Tim Webb, Channel Four Televison

  *Introducing real people: understanding Asperger syndrome*  Essex County Council

*Available from NAS Publications
Tel: 020 7033 9237
Fax: 020 7739 8479
Or order online at www.autism.org.uk/pubs

# appendix 1
# visual prompt sheet.....

The visual prompt sheet is designed to support the pupil in recognising the relevant information in the lesson. The sheet should be completed by the teacher prior to the lesson and then given to the pupil at the start of the lesson. If this sheet was produced as an OHT it could be used to support all pupils.

The following sheet 'Help yourself to learn' is a suggested format and may be copied or adapted for your use.

# help yourself to learn!

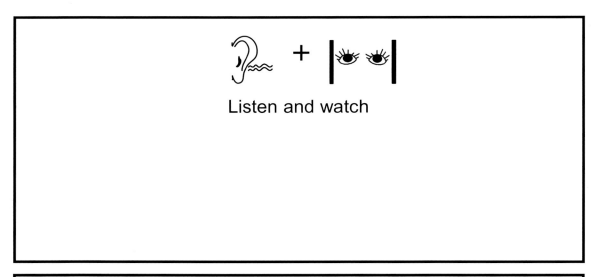

Listen and watch

Spellings

Write

# appendix 2
# concept maps....

## What are they?

Concept mapping is widely used in primary and secondary schools as a learning tool. The maps help learners make explicit to themselves and to others how they view the relationships between associated words, concepts and ideas.

Learners record connections between concepts by joining them and explaining the nature of the association. Such maps can be used to provide an insight into how the learner thinks about a scientific idea.

This is an example of a concept map provided by Steve Edwards, KS3 Science Consultant.

**Main theme**: respiratory system

**Connect with**: energy release, respiration, chemical reaction, movement, glucose, oxygen.

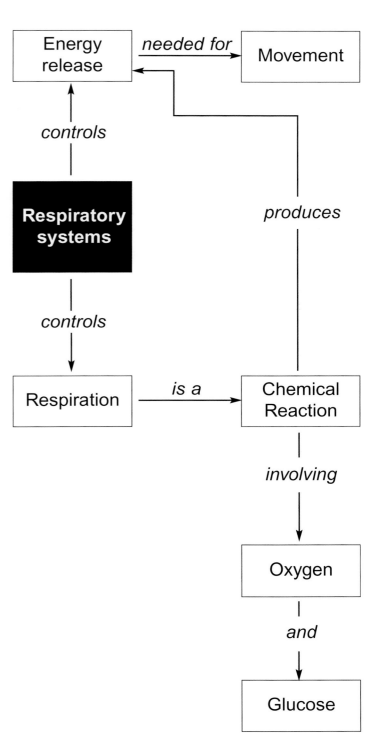

Social Stories™ were devised by Carol Gray (1991) to help students with autism in their understanding of social situations. Social Stories™ have also been effective with pupils with learning, emotional or behavioural difficulties, where inappropriate behaviours have arisen from an impaired understanding of the social context. Social Stories™ are often written in response to a troubling situation, in an effort to provide the pupils with the social information they may be lacking.

*At least 50% of all Social Stories™ developed for a specific child, adolescent or adult with ASD must applaud what that person currently does well.

A Social Story™ informs and may advise the pupil about a social situation. It focuses on the relevant, idiosyncratic and immediate social difficulties being experienced by the pupil.

Effective features of Social Stories™:

- **visual** – presented in a written form with photos, drawings, symbols or a diagram
- **permanent** – the child can read the Social Story™ over and over again
- **written in simple language** – the Social Story™ reflects the pupil's language and vocabulary
- **based on observations** – observations of the pupil, discussions with the pupil and information from those who know the pupil best
- **explicit** – the Social Story™ makes explicit the rules, expectations and codes of behaviour which are often implicit or assumed
- **factual** – it offers the pupil information about who is doing what and why
- **thoughts and feelings** – it often focuses on what people are thinking and feeling and how that relates to their behaviour
- **situation specific**
- **written in a predictable style.**

**Reference:** *Gray, C (2002) *My Social Stories Book*. London: Jessica Kingsley Publications. www.thegraycenter.org

*Available from NAS Publications 020 7903 3595
www.autism.org.uk/pubs

# guidelines to writing a Social Story™....

Observe the targeted situation. This includes where and when the situation occurs, who is involved, how events are sequenced, what occurs and why. Talk to all staff involved and, if appropriate, the parents.

Compare your story to the list below, and tick off all the points that apply. If 1-10 describe the story you have developed, it's a Social Story™.

1. The story meaningfully shares social information with an overall patient and reassuring quality. (If this is a story teaching a new concept or skill, another is developed to praise a child's positive qualities, behaviors, or achievements.)

2. The story has an introduction that clearly identifies the topic, a body that adds detail and a conclusion that reinforces and summarizes the information.

3. The story provides answers to "wh" questions, describing the setting or context (WHERE), time-related information (WHEN), relevant people (WHO), important cues (WHAT), basic activities, behaviors, or statements (HOW), and the reasons or rationale behind them (WHY).

4. The story is written from a first person perspective, as though the child is describing the event (most often for a younger or more severely challenged child) or third person perspective, like a newspaper article (usually for a more advanced child, or an adolescent or adult).

5. The story uses positive language, omitting descriptions or references to challenging behaviours in favor of identifying positive responses.

6. The story consists of descriptive sentences (objective, often observable, statements of fact), with an option of any one or more of the following sentence types:
   ● perspective sentences, that describe the thoughts, feelings, and/or beliefs of other people co-operative sentences to explain what others will do in support of the child
   ● directive sentences that identify suggested responses or choices of responses to a given situation
   ● affirmative sentences that enhance the meaning of surrounding statements
   ● and/or control sentences, developed by the child to help him/her recall and apply information in the story.

7. Appendix A: The Social Story™ Checklist
   Directions: Compare your story to the list below, and check off all that apply.
   If 1-10 describe the story you have developed, it's a Social Story™.

8. The story matches the ability and interests of the audience, and is literally accurate (exception: if analogies and/or metaphors are used).

9. If appropriate, the story uses carefully selected illustrations that are meaningful for the child and enhance the meaning of the text.

10. The title of the story meets all applicable Social Story™ criteria.

- The story meaningfully shares social information with an overall patient and reassuring quality. (If this is a story teaching a new concept or skill, another is developed another to praise a child's positive qualities, behaviors, or achievements.)

- The story has an introduction that clearly identifies the topic, a body that adds detail, and a conclusion that reinforces and summarizes the information.

- The story provides answers to "wh" questions, describing the setting or context (WHERE), time-related information (WHEN), relevant people (WHO), important cues (WHAT), basic activities, behaviors, or statements (HOW), and the reasons or rationale behind them (WHY).

- The story is written from a first person perspective, as though the child is describing the event (most often for a younger or more severely challenged child, or third person perspective, like a newspaper article (usually for a more advanced child, or an adolescent or adult).

- The story uses positive language, omitting descriptions or references to challenging behaviors in favor of identifying positive responses.

- The story is comprised of descriptive sentences (objective, often observable, statements of fact), with an option of any one or more of the following sentence types: perspective sentences (that describe the thoughts, feelings, and/or beliefs of other people); cooperative sentences (to explain what others will do in support of the child); directive sentences (that identify suggested responses or choices of responses to a given situation); affirmative sentences (that enhance the meaning of surrounding statements); and/or control sentences (developed by the child to help him/her recall and apply information in the story).

- The story follows the Social Story Formula:

$$\frac{\text{DESCRIBE (descriptive + perspective + Cooperative + affirmative sentences)}}{\text{*DIRECT (directive + control sentences)}} \geq 2$$

*If there are no directive and/or control sentences, use 1 instead of 0 as the denominator.

- The story matches the ability and interests of the audience, and is literally accurate (exception: if analogies and/or metaphors are used).

- If appropriate, the story uses carefully selected illustrations that are meaningful for the child and enhance the meaning of the text.

- The title of the story meets all applicable Social Story™ criteria.

Restricted permission is granted to copy this checklist for non-profit home, school, and therapeutic use.

26

While some pupils with an ASD may be good readers in that they have excellent decoding skills and a good sight vocabulary, they may find it difficult to make sense of what they are reading (hyperlexia).

Such pupils may read the subject words but find it difficult to interpret what they need (books and equipment) for each lesson.

The visual timetable on the next page is an example of one prepared for a high functioning pupil with an ASD by Nicola Griffiths, Special Needs Support Assistant at Chipping Sodbury High School.

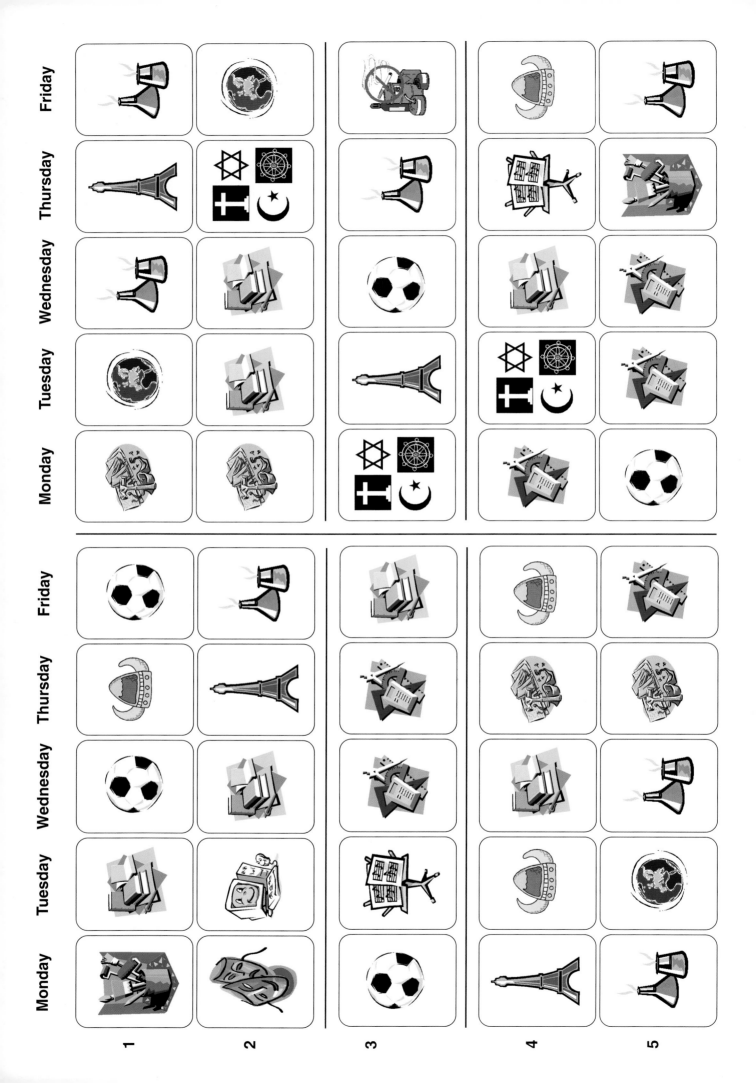

# appendix 5
# circle of friends....

Circle of Friends is a strategy developed in Canada to promote the inclusion of pupils with special educational needs in mainstream settings. This approach has been implemented in Nottingham, Leicestershire, Bristol and elsewhere in the UK. It has been shown to be particularly helpful in promoting the inclusion of pupils with an ASD.

A circle is made up of six to eight pupils from the tutor group who meet weekly with the focus child and an adult. The circle aims to:

- acknowledge the focus pupil's strengths and progress
- identify difficulties
- determine targets and strategies to address difficulties identified by the pupils.
- put into practice their ideas and review.

**Reference:**

Colin Newton and Derek Wilson (1999) *Circles of friends.* London: Folens

Whitaker et al (1998) 'Children with autism and peer group support: using circles of friends,' *British Journal of Special Education.*

www.inclusive-solutions.com/circlesoffriends.asp

# appendix 6
# visual scripts....

This visual approach aims to develop pupils' skills in responding more appropriately in social situations. The mentor, in discussion with the pupil with an ASD, identifies situations that may cause difficulties. They work together to produce a visual script, which reminds the pupil of a more common and appropriate response to a situation.

Below are two examples produced by Terry Whyton, teacher from the Learning Support Department in Marlwood School, South Gloucestershire.

# appendix 7
# analysing the function of behaviour using
# STAR approach....

**STAR** stands for
**S**etting **T**rigger **A**ctions **R**esults

For some pupils with an ASD, challenging behaviours should be regarded as responses to situations and demands. This may be ways of gaining attention, expressing feelings, expressing needs or refusing.

## What are settings?
Settings can be environmental or personal. They are the contexts in which actions occur.

## Environmental setting conditions include:
- the physical aspects of the pupil's environment
- the social interactions within that environment
- the activities provided for the pupil.

## Personal setting conditions include:
- the pupil's physical well being
- the pupil's psychological state
- the pupil's thoughts and moods.

## What are triggers?
Triggers occur just before the action. They are the signals that 'set off' the specific actions, eg the teacher putting pen in her briefcase may signal the end of the lesson.

## What are actions?
Actions are observable behaviours. The STAR approach starts by analysing the action describing the behaviour accurately, eg The pupil ran out of the changing room before a games lesson.

## What are the results?
Results follow an action. Results influence the chance of a pupil repeating that action on other occasions.

# Using STAR approach to manage a challenging behaviour.

**A scenario:** The art teacher asks pupils to work in partnership to produce a collage.

## What are the actions?

- The pupil refuses to move from his seat.

## What are the settings?

- **Environmental** – Noisy, hot, pupils sitting in different places.
- **Personal** – The pupil always chooses to sit in a particular place and feels calm in this position.

## What are the triggers?

The teacher directed the pupils to work as partners.

## What are the results?

The teacher repeats the instruction and the child becomes agitated.

- The function of the action was to express that he wanted to stay in his seat.

- Consider altering the environmental settings – prepare the pupil by asking the partner to move to sit next to the pupil.

- Make it optional to allow a pupil to work on his own.

## The STAR approach will help to

- describe the challenging behaviour objectively

- focus on the function the behaviour has

- look at the setting, the potential triggers and the results

- to change the behaviour the adult can alter the settings, manipulate the trigger or teach an alternative action

- remember to reward any appropriate behaviour immediately.

# STAR approach

Name:

Date:

| Settings | Triggers | Actions | Results |
|----------|----------|---------|---------|
|          |          |         |         |

**Can you alter –**
setting, triggers, actions, results.

# Notes

# Notes